OLD BEN FRANKLIN'S PHILADELPHIA

brimmed with excitement on May 13, 1787, for General George Washington was coming to town! All Philadelphia turned out to greet the Revolutionary War hero, who would attend the important meetings of the Constitutional Convention. Philadelphians greeted Washington with the new flag of the United States—red, white, and blue, with thirteen stars, one for each new state.

While he waited for the other delegates to arrive, Washington made himself at home in the fashionable city. He saw Philadelphia's beautiful houses and dined in formal splendor in gracious dining rooms. He visited Ben Franklin's home, enjoyed his warm hospitality, and saw the many "contrivances" Franklin had invented.

These early days during the founding of our country were busy ones in Franklin's thriving and fascinating hometown. Old Philadelphia comes alive in this book, which is illustrated with paintings, old engravings, and prints.

This is one of the *How They Lived* series, developed by Garrard to give meaning to the study of American history. Young people will find a deeper understanding and more lasting appreciation of history and geography as they see life of the past through the eyes of those who lived it.

Old Ben Franklin's Philadelphia

Old Ben Franklin's Philadelphia

BY ELIZABETH RIDER MONTGOMERY

ILLUSTRATED BY HERMAN B. VESTAL

GARRARD PUBLISHING COMPANY
CHAMPAIGN, ILLINOIS

For Lisa Phillips

Picture credits:

American Numismatic Society: p. 21
American Philosophical Society Library, Philadelphia: p. 10, 18, 40, 71, 74
The Franklin Institute: p. 14, 19
Historical Society of Pennsylvania: p. 82
Independence National Historical Park Collection: p. 89
Insurance Company of North America, Philadelphia: p. 1, 32, 80, 81, 84, 85
John Carter Brown Library, Brown University: p. 91
Library of Congress: p. 5, 24, 25, 26, 31, 66
The Mariners Museum, Newport News, Virginia: p. 34
The Metropolitan Museum of Art, Bequest of Charles Allen Munn, 1924: p. 22
The Metropolitan Museum of Art, Rogers Fund, 1942: p. 37, 39, 53
National Gallery of Art, Gift of Edgar William and Bernice Chrysler Garbisch: p. 58
Pennsylvania Academy of the Fine Arts: p. 46, 76, 93
Prints Division, New York Public Library: p. 2, 30, 33, 69
Rare Book Division, New York Public Library: p. 35, 49
Shelburne Museum, Inc., Staff Photographer Einars J. Mengis: p. 48

Endsheets: *The City of Philadelphia in Pennsylvania*
            I. N. Phelps Stokes Collection
            New York Public Library

Contents

1. A Welcome for the General

Philadelphia was usually quiet on Sundays in 1787, except for the morning clamor of church bells. Families walked to church and strolled slowly home again for a quiet dinner. All shops were closed. The streets were empty of carriages and horses.

However, the Sunday afternoon of May 13 was different. Crowds of people lined Philadelphia's main street. Shouts and cheers filled the spring air. Children laughed and clapped.

The bells of Christ Church rang out, although it was long past church time. Drums rolled and fifes squealed. Carriage wheels creaked and groaned. Horses' hooves clattered on the cobblestones. The boots of blue-coated soldiers thumped out a steady marching rhythm.

The General was coming! General George Washington was coming! All of Philadelphia turned out to welcome the man who had led the American armies to victory in the War for Independence. He had come to Philadelphia to attend a most important meeting. As they cheered, people waved the new American flag. It was a red and white striped flag with thirteen white stars in a circle on a blue field.

Washington's carriage came to a halt at the corner of Fifth and High Streets. He intended to stay at a boarding house there.

A great crowd waited. Tall and strong, calm and dignified, George Washington climbed down a bit stiffly from his carriage. It had been a long, tiring trip. With a wave of his big hand he acknowledged the cheers of the people.

Robert Morris pushed through the crowd to greet him. Plump and red-faced, this wealthy Philadelphia merchant looked very elegant in his rich plum-colored suit.

"You will lodge at no boarding house, my friend," Morris told Washington. "Mrs. Morris and I insist that you shall be our guest during your stay in Philadelphia."

Washington smiled at his old friend. Morris took the General's arm in a firm grip. He led him to his home at 190 High Street, where Mrs. Morris greeted Washington cordially.

Washington had not been inside this house before, for Morris had bought it only two years earlier. It was one of the finest houses in the city, a handsome three-story brick, with

This view of Robert Morris' house was drawn a few
years after the Constitutional Convention.

small-paned windows and white shutters. Like
most Philadelphia houses, it was built close to
the street, with no front lawn whatever. There
was a fine marble doorstep, with an iron
footscraper that everyone was supposed to use
before going inside.

On the first floor of the house were the
family living and dining rooms. An elegant
staircase led from the big entrance hall to
spacious drawing rooms upstairs used for
entertaining. Some of the walls were covered
with expensive French wallpaper, which had
just become fashionable. This must have

10

interested Washington, because he had recently ordered wallpaper for his home at Mount Vernon.

The floors were covered with thick carpets. Only rich people could afford these. Most people had to be content with sanded floors, but many did not like carpets anyway. Carpets caught dirt and could not be easily cleaned. A sanded floor, on the other hand, could be swept and scrubbed every day, covered with fresh sand, and there was a spanking clean floor!

The pleasant bedroom that Mrs. Morris had assigned to Washington had a big fireplace. So did every other room in the house, for a fireplace was the only source of heat. The bedroom had a big bed with curtains around it to keep out the cold. It also had a commode, or washstand, with a marble top, holding a large washbowl and a pitcher of water. Behind the door in the commode was a slop jar that a servant emptied every day.

Washington washed his hands and face at once, to remove the dust of his five-day journey.

Meanwhile, his carriage had been taken through the alley to Robert Morris' coach

house, which had a stable big enough for twelve horses.

The backyard included a big lawn, beautiful gardens, and a fine orchard. There was also a place to hang clothes to dry, and probably a toolhouse and a woodhouse. Undoubtedly there was also a "necessary," or toilet, although some Philadelphia houses had the "necessary" in the cellar. The big backyard was enclosed by a high brick wall.

Servants began to unload the General's bags and boxes and carry them into the house and up the back stairs. They went past the big washhouse, the huge kitchen, and the "bathing room."

We do not know why this small room was called the "bathing room," for there was no inside plumbing at that time, and there were no real bathtubs. A few years later, after George Washington had become the first President of the United States, he lived in the Morris house. Then a copper bathtub was installed. It was probably filled and emptied by the servants, for piped-in water was rare indeed.

Now while his servants unpacked his clothes and hung them in the clothespress, or wardrobe, Washington brushed his suit carefully. He was getting ready to call on the man whom he considered to be the "wisest living American." That evening George Washington wrote in his diary: "As soon as I got to town, I waited on the President (of Pennsylvania), Dr. Franklin."

Benjamin Franklin plays the "armonica," the musical
instrument which he invented.

2. Two Great Americans

Benjamin Franklin, the President of Pennsylvania, sat in his favorite armchair in his upstairs library, reading.

There was not another chair exactly like it in the world, for Franklin had designed it himself. Above the chair was fastened a large fan that could be moved back and forth with a foot pedal. As he read, Franklin could fan himself and keep off flies at the same time, merely by moving his foot a trifle.

Although Franklin had spent much time abroad as a representative of his country, Philadelphia had been his home for more than

60 years. Now past 80, in almost constant pain, Franklin did not look at all like "the wisest living American." He was a plain-looking, stout old man, dressed in a brown suit.

Franklin "wore his own hair." That is, he did not wear a wig, and he did not powder his hair. The thin, straight gray locks hung down over his large head to his neck and looked most unfashionable. But Franklin's mind was just as active as it had been in his youth, his smile as ready and warm, his sense of humor just as strong. He loved to joke. His eyes sparkled brightly behind the bifocal glasses that he had invented for both near and far vision.

His young granddaughter Deborah ran into the room.

"Grandpapa!" she cried. "General Washington is here!"

Franklin hugged the little girl fondly. Ever since the death of his wife, his daughter and her family had lived with him. He loved his grandchildren dearly, and they adored him.

"Ask the General to be good enough to come upstairs," he told the child.

When George Washington was shown into the library, Franklin took up his walking stick

and tried to rise, but Washington would not
let him. He knew how painful it was for the
old man to stand.

These two great Americans had not met since
the early days of the war. Now the meeting
between them was very warm. Each had great
respect for the other. Both had worked hard
to help their country win its independence
from England. Washington had led the soldiers
on the battlefield. Franklin had made friends
in France, where he obtained help for the new
United States of America.

Washington looked around Franklin's big

library. The walls were entirely filled with books from the floor to the high ceiling. Franklin had thousands of books—the biggest private library in America.

The old man showed his friend many of his inventions, which he called "contrivances." Washington had already seen the Franklin stove, which was like a movable fireplace. It warmed a room better than a regular fireplace and burned far less wood. This stove is still in common use today.

Washington also knew about two other popular inventions of Franklin's, the lightning rod and the "armonica," or musical glasses.

Franklin often used this chair as a ladder to reach the upper shelves in his library.

This lightning rod is believed to be one of the earliest ones made by Benjamin Franklin.

But he had not seen Franklin's new invention, a rolling press for making copies of letters. Undoubtedly the General wished he had one. He had learned long ago that it was wise to keep copies of the letters he sent. A press like this would save a great deal of time.

Benjamin Franklin demonstrated the use of his "artificial arm," with which he could take books down from the highest shelf. He also showed his friend a chair that became a step-ladder when the seat was lifted. Both of these Franklin "contrivances" are in common use today, especially in libraries.

Dr. Franklin surely showed Washington his

electrical apparatus and other scientific machines. Both men belonged to the American Philosophical Society whose members exchanged information on science. Franklin had founded the Society years before.

Washington may have noticed that the doors in Franklin's house were edged with heavy cloth to prevent noise and keep out drafts. He may have seen the old man's clever "contrivance" for bolting his bedroom door without getting out of bed, and his method of reviving a dying fire without bending over the fireplace. Later that summer Washington wrote in his diary that he had seen an ironing machine at Franklin's home, which the inventor called a "mangle." Without doubt, Benjamin Franklin was one of the most inventive men in America!

George Washington must have examined Franklin's house and his "contrivances" with deep interest. He was always looking for ways to make his beloved Mount Vernon more comfortable and more beautiful. Franklin was glad to have other people copy his ideas. He would never patent any of his inventions.

However, the two old friends surely spent most of this visit talking about the meeting

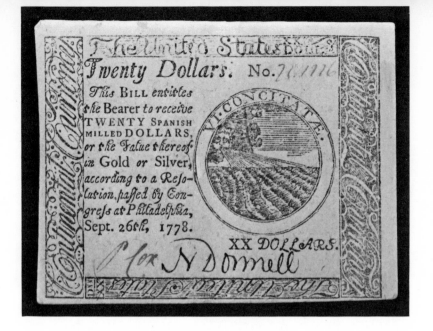

This bill was almost worthless because it promised the bearer coins which Congress did not have.

that had brought Washington to Philadelphia, the Constitutional Convention.

When the American Revolution ended, the thirteen United States were independent at last. But they were not really united. Each state considered itself a nation. They were jealous of each other, and they quarreled among themselves. Virginia and Pennsylvania quarreled over boundaries. New York and Connecticut threatened war against each other over a tax on firewood and farm produce.

There was no strong central government. The Continental Congress could not levy taxes. It could print paper money, but its money was

Hungry and ragged soldiers huddled around campfires
for warmth during the bitter winter at Valley Forge.

nearly worthless. It could make laws, but it could not carry them out.

Nobody knew better than George Washington how helpless the Continental Congress was. During the war he had written hundreds of letters to the Congress asking for arms, shoes, and food for his starving soldiers, but Congress had sent him very little. Washington doubted that he could have won the war if Robert Morris had not supplied his army with ammunition and other necessities.

Men like Washington, Franklin, Madison, and

Hamilton knew that the thirteen weak, separate states could not survive. In order to become a strong nation, the states must band together and work hard for the independence of the new nation.

So the Constitutional Convention had been called to draw up a plan that would strengthen the central government. Delegates had been elected in each state, except Rhode Island, to attend the Convention. It was to begin the next day.

"It will be a pleasure to work with you in this Convention," Washington told Benjamin Franklin, and Franklin returned the compliment to the General.

3. The "Terrible Traffic" of 1787

The next morning George Washington rose early as usual. When breakfast was over, he set out for the State House where the meeting would be held. Robert Morris was also a delegate to the Constitutional Convention, but he must attend to business first.

It was only two blocks from the Morris home to the State House (shown above). However, Washington liked to walk around the city, so he probably went several blocks out of his way.

Philadelphia was a busy, noisy city. Carriages clattered on the cobblestones, taking wealthy businessmen like Robert Morris to their offices. Heavy wagons rumbled toward the docks, where sailing ships waited for their cargoes. Horses neighed. Drivers shouted. Pigs squealed and ran from screeching wheels. Children shouted and laughed on their way to school.

The din was terrific. People who wanted to talk had to step inside a tavern or a shop in order to hear each other's words.

"What terrible traffic!" people complained. "Did you ever in your life see so many horses and carriages?"

This view of Market and Second Street was engraved by William Birch a few years after the Convention.

Vendors set up shop, and farmers sell produce to the
hurrying passers-by in the business district.

Then somebody was sure to reply, "One
thing is certain: Traffic is as bad as it can
possibly get."

Philadelphia streets were the same level as
the brick sidewalks, called "pavements." There
were no curbs. Strong cedar posts were placed
along the edge of the sidewalks to keep horses
off so pedestrians would not be hurt.

The pavements swarmed with people. Carpenters, bricklayers, and painters hurried along,
carrying the tools of their trade. Apprentice
boys pushed wheelbarrows, piled high with
paper for a printshop, or bright cloth for a
tailor shop, or beaver skins for a hat shop.

26

The young apprentices often stopped to talk to the servant girls drawing water at the public pumps. There was a pump of good water every hundred yards or so.

Philadelphia, halfway between Maine and Georgia, was now the greatest city in America. More than 40,000 people lived there. One traveler wrote:

> "No other city could boast of so many streets, so many houses, so many people, so much renown. No other city was so rich, so extravagant, so fashionable."

Yes, Washington might have thought as he walked, Philadelphia was all those things. But it was not clean or quiet or restful.

Trash and garbage were thrown into the streets. There wasn't any sewage or garbage disposal then. Pigs were allowed to run in the streets, and they ate the refuse. The smells of garbage, sewage, and horse manure mingled to make a mighty stench.

In summer the unpaved streets were inches deep in dust. Washington was glad for the long spell of rainy weather that kept the dust down. But the mud that replaced the dust, especially through the winter, was even worse. Then the streets would be so mucky that a gentleman would mount his horse merely to cross the street, to avoid wading in the mud. A lady was usually carried from her coach to her front door.

From the time Benjamin Franklin was a young man, he had tried to get the people of Philadelphia to pave its streets and to light them. Some of the streets were now paved with cobblestones, and a few were lighted at night with lanterns.

If Philadelphia streets were dirty, the marble doorsteps of the houses were not. Every morning the doorstep of each house in town must be scrubbed. This was an invariable custom. Visitors walking down the streets early in the morning were often amazed at the sight of Philadelphia housewives or their servants on their knees scrubbing the marble steps. One visitor said it looked as if they were all at prayer.

Another Philadelphia custom concerned those same front steps. On hot summer evenings a young lady would dress up and sit on a bench by her front doorstep to keep cool. The young

men of the city would walk from one doorstep
to another, visiting with the lovely girls.

Usually Philadelphia women were kept busy
indoors. But they could see what was happen-
ing in the street without going outside. Most
houses had a double-paned mirror, called a
"busybody," fastened to a windowsill. By
looking in the "busybody," the housewife could
see what was going on outside without being
seen.

No doubt many women and girls watched
the straight, soldierly General striding along
the street that morning. George Washington
probably walked down to the riverfront to set

his big pocketwatch by the great clock on the dock. He liked to do this every day.

Philadelphia was more than 100 miles from the ocean. This was too far for any salt air or sea breeze to reach the city, but in every other way Philadelphia was an ocean port. Ships came up the Delaware River to unload goods from Europe, the West Indies, and the Orient. Washington could have seen as many as 100 ships tied up at the long wharves, or sailing up or down the river. Some of them probably belonged to his host, Robert Morris.

Plan of the City of Philadelphia by William Birch.
1. Robert Morris' house, 2. Benjamin Franklin's house,
3. The State House, 4. Wharves, 5. Marketplace.

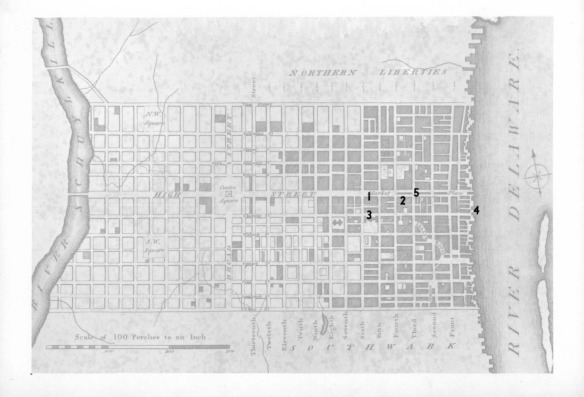

Busy stevedores unload ships at Arch Street Ferry.

Workmen in leather aprons carried boxes and bales down the gangplanks and piled them on the pavements. Other men loaded them on wagons, to be taken to Philadelphia warehouses and stores, or to other parts of Pennsylvania. Ships' officers bawled out orders at the tops of their voices. Workmen shouted and joked as they labored. Horses pawed the cobblestones restlessly as they waited for their wagons to be loaded. Anchor chains rattled, winches creaked, wheels screeched.

Big wagons brought goods to be shipped out. Here was a wagon packed carefully with fine furniture. There was one stacked high with crates of live chickens and another loaded with new lumber. Other wagons carried hats, shoes,

31

books, tools, as well as foot stoves which people sometimes carried to church.

When a ship's cargo was safely stowed on board and its supplies of food and water loaded, the ship set sail if the tide was high. It would sail down the Delaware River and out to the Atlantic Ocean. Months would pass before it would complete its voyage and return to the great inland port of Philadelphia.

Along the waterfront were many business houses and shops to serve sailors and ship-owners. There were taverns, coffeehouses, warehouses, and a customshouse. There were also many shops for outfitting ships with such items

These ships sailed up the Delaware and anchored near the bustling inland port of Philadelphia.

The frigate *Philadelphia* is being built and will be
outfitted in this busy Philadelphia shipyard.

as ropes, sails, riggings, and cabinets. So many
ships were outfitted in the port of Philadelphia,
that a common saying ran, "The ship has a
Boston bottom and a Philadelphia top."

Washington did not need his eyes to locate
the fish markets. They could be found by the
sense of smell, and there were many of them.
If the main business section of Philadelphia
had seemed odorous to Washington, the waterfront reeked! The smells of decaying fish,
drainage ditches, and the usual street smells of
horses and ancient garbage combined with the
odor of old ships, new lumber, tar, and rope.

George Washington probably enjoyed looking

in the shops of the figurehead carvers. In those days, each ship carried a figurehead fastened to its prow. It might be a likeness of a person or an animal or a fanciful figure. Some of the finest artists in Philadelphia carved figureheads for ships.

Washington was interested in the work of artists, because several had painted his picture recently. He did not know that many more artists would paint his portrait in years to come, while he served as President of the United States!

4. Trials in Traveling

When George Washington reached the State House after his roundabout walk, he was annoyed to learn that the meeting could not begin that day. Only the Pennsylvania and Virginia delegates were present. No delegates had yet arrived from the other states. Always prompt himself, Washington resented tardiness.

Benjamin Franklin, however, was cheerful about the delay. The wise old man was seldom upset.

He had been carried over to the State House in his sedan chair, a strong, covered chair fastened to two long bars, held carefully by two of his servants. Now that he was old and in constant pain, Franklin found a sedan chair more comfortable than a jolting carriage.

James Madison of Virginia was also cheerful about the delay. "Remember the long spell of bad weather we have had," he reminded his friends. "Every road is a muddy mirror."

George Washington knew this was true. It had taken him almost five full days to travel from Mount Vernon to Philadelphia, less than 150 miles away.

In those days, rich people traveled in their own coaches or on horseback. Poorer people rode in their wagons or in public stagecoaches or they walked.

Washington had traveled to Philadelphia in his own carriage, drawn by four horses. He had skirted mudholes and crossed swollen streams. He had been jolted and jounced by deep ruts in the road. He had ridden long hours every day, from dawn to dark. Although his servants drove and cared for the horses, Washington had been tired when he finished his journey. Even so, the trip was far more comfortable than it would have been in a public stagecoach.

In 1810, stagecoach passengers were still jolted on rough roads. Painting by Pavel Svinin, a Russian.

Stagecoaches at that time were merely big wagons with straight sides. They had three or four benches, without backs. When a passenger got on, he had to climb over the front benches to get to the rear seats. The back seat was most prized, because passengers could lean against the back of the wagon.

There was little room for baggage in a stage. One traveler said that an American took on a trip "only a comb, a razor, and a couple of shirts and cravats."

As a rule four horses drew the stage. Several times a day the stage stopped at an inn or wayside station to exchange the tired horses for fresh ones. Some drivers did not change horses often enough. They drove their horses until they dropped.

Most roads were little more than rough trails, with deep ruts and gullies. Sometimes there were chasms several feet deep! Since the wagons had no springs, the passengers were severely jolted as the wagons lurched over those "bone-shaking" roads.

A stagecoach driver had to know every part of the road. In rainy weather the mud might be so deep in places that the stage would sink to the axles. The driver had to know when to stop so the passengers could get out and push.

Sometimes a stage would be in danger of overturning, and the driver would tell his passengers to lean to the right to keep the stage on an even keel. A few minutes later he might call out, "Now, gentlemen, to the left!"

In spite of the drivers' care and skill, many stages overturned in the mud. Sometimes the horses would get loose and run away.

In summer the dust on the roads might be a foot deep. The travelers' bright-colored clothes were soon so dust-covered that they seemed to be all the same color.

Bridges were often nothing more than heavy planks set on top of two logs. The driver usually had to stop his stage before crossing a stream and set the planks in place.

Few rivers had bridges however. Most of them were crossed by means of ferries or boats. Sometimes the ferry was a large, flat-bottomed boat that carried the stage, horses, passengers, and all. But many times the passengers left the stage behind when they boarded the boat. After crossing the river they got on another stage.

Boatmen ferried these travelers, carriage and all, across a river in this Svinin painting.

John Fitch's steamboat chugs up the Delaware River
close to the city of Philadelphia.

Boats had no engines at that time. But later
that summer, for the first time in history, a
boat would go against the current on the
Delaware River under its own power. The boat
was a steamboat made by John Fitch, and
some of the Constitutional Convention delegates
would ride in it.

Most ferries were pulled across the river by
means of a rope. Others were pushed with long
poles, called "setting poles." Once in a while a
ferry was so heavily loaded that there was
only an inch or two between the deck of the
boat and the water. Then the passengers would
wonder if they would get across at all!

A fast stagecoach line ran between New York City and Philadelphia. It covered more than 90 miles in a day, but it was a long, long day. The fare was six dollars.

Alexander Hamilton, a delegate from New York, would probably have traveled by this stage, which crossed four streams on ferries. The evening before he wanted to take the stage, Hamilton would have had to take a boat from New York City to Perth Amboy on the New Jersey shore. There he would spend the night. The next morning he would be awakened at three o'clock. He would get up in the dark, dress quickly, and hurry out to get on the stage. Several hours would pass before the stage stopped at an inn to change horses and let the passengers eat breakfast. Alexander Hamilton was surely famished by then!

There was so much travel in and out of Philadelphia in those days that many inns or hotels had been built. An inn was often called a "tavern" or an "ordinary."

An inn served many purposes. The stage horses were changed there. Inns also provided rooms and meals for the weary travelers. For meals, all the guests sat around one big table. The food was set out and each person ate all he wanted. The price was the same, whether he ate a single slice of ham or beef, or three or four servings of every single dish.

Some inns could give each traveler a private room, but usually several strangers had to room together or even sleep in the same bed. When all the beds were filled, sometimes five or six to a bed, travelers would sleep on the floor of the inn's taproom in front of the huge fireplace. As many as 100 sometimes slept on the floor of one big tavern.

Good taverns came to be the landmarks of a journey. Instead of speaking of the distance between towns, travelers spoke of the distance between certain taverns.

Inns not only served travelers. They were important to the people who lived nearby as well.

Taverns sometimes served as post offices. When the postrider passed, he would throw a bundle of letters on a table or counter in the inn. The letters might lie there for days before the owners claimed them. They would be handled and examined by the curious, who might even read them! Reading other people's mail was so common that Thomas Jefferson wrote in code to his friends.

Some letters were never claimed. After a certain time they were sent to the "dead letter office," which Benjamin Franklin had started during the years he served as postmaster general for the colonies.

Mail was slow and uncertain. There were few newspapers and most of them were weeklies. Even the *Pennsylvania Packet*, one of the first daily newspapers in the United States, could not carry up-to-date news. There was no way of getting news quickly, since there were no telephones, telegraphs, or radios. When travelers arrived at an inn, therefore, local citizens would hurry over to hear news of the outside world.

Inns soon became meeting places for local people. Lectures, exhibits, and entertainments were held in them. Washington might have seen at Philadelphia taverns that summer a wild animal show, a puppet show, a balloon ascension, an auction, and a demonstration of electricity, besides hearing a concert and a lecture.

Philadelphia men had taken to meeting their friends in their favorite taverns for dinner or supper. These groups sometimes became regular clubs. The most famous of these clubs was

called the "Junto." Benjamin Franklin had
formed it when he was a very young man.
It met regularly for more than 30 years.

During the months of the Constitutional
Convention's meetings, James Madison, Alexander Hamilton, and others stayed at the
Indian Queen Tavern around the corner from
Franklin's home. Several delegates often gath-
ered at a tavern for dinner. George Washington wrote in his diary about many of these
dinners.

5. Gay Dress and Gray Dress

Every day George Washington, Benjamin Franklin, James Madison, and their friends went to the State House. Every day a few more delegates appeared, but not enough for the Convention to begin its work.

Washington became a familiar figure in Philadelphia, taking his morning walk from the Morris home to the State House. Tall and powerful, he looked very impressive in his long blue coat and smart cocked hat. His knee breeches were fastened with silver buckles. He wore stylish long silk stockings, held in place with ribbon garters. There were shining silver buttons on his coat and silver buckles on his square-toed shoes.

Many people wore wigs. Even children wore them. But Washington did not. He powdered his hair and tied it in a queue. This fashion of powdered hair was not as expensive as wigs, and it was not as hot and uncomfortable. But it was hard on clothes. The hair was oiled to make the powder stick, and both oil and powder rubbed off on the clothes.

During the two weeks that Washington, Franklin, Madison, and the others waited for the Constitutional Convention to start, they were invited to many dinner parties, teas, and balls. Mr. and Mrs. Morris gave parties for the delegates, and so did the mayor of Philadelphia.

Franklin, old and ill, did not go to many parties, but Washington went everywhere and enjoyed everything. He saw that he would need more clothes, so he wrote home asking for "my blue coat with the crimson collar, and also my new umbrella."

When he dressed for a ball, George Washington looked very grand indeed. He wore satin or velvet breeches, a waistcoat, and a long satin coat. His shirt had wide lace cuffs and

This European fashion doll was dressed in the latest style.

lace ruffles down the front. He always wore his sword to parties, even when dancing.

Like most Philadelphians, Washington loved to dance. Their favorite dances were the stately minuet and the quadrille. These would seem very slow to us, but fast dances would have been impossible for men wearing swords and women wearing hoopskirts.

Philadelphia women loved fine clothes and bright colors. There were no fashion magazines then, and no ready-to-wear clothes. To keep up with the fashions, a lady like Mrs. Morris would order each year from Europe a

48

doll dressed in the latest style. Then she would have her own clothes made in a similar fashion. She would have her hair dressed in a high, stiffened headdress, like the doll's.

For days before a ball, the tailors, dressmakers, and milliners of Philadelphia would be very busy. On the day of the party, the hairdressers would be busiest of all. Some ladies would have to have their mountainous hair styles done the day before. They would have to sleep sitting up and move carefully all day long, for fear the towering mass of hair might fall down.

A Philadelphia dressmaker fits a gown for a fashionable lady in this old print.

A portrait of Mrs. Morris painted about this
time shows her hair done in an elaborate
structure a foot high and a foot wide. The
hair is topped with waving plumes and encir-
cled with a wide ribbon.

At the ball, a Philadelphia lady would be
gorgeous indeed. Her wide, floor-length gown
of silk, satin, velvet, or brocade had hoopskirts
inside it to hold it out at the sides. She wore
satin slippers and carried a fan. Usually a
servant followed her, carrying her wrap and
powder. The light from hundreds of candles
revealed the whiteness of the lady's face and

arms, for she always wore a linen mask and long gloves whenever she went out in the sun. No lady would dream of letting her skin become tanned!

At some balls, a private room was prepared for Quaker ladies. There were many Quakers in Philadelphia, for the city had been founded by a Quaker, William Penn. Their religion did not allow them to dance or go to the theater. But Quaker ladies might go to a ball and sit in a separate room, out of sight. They watched the dancing and entertainment through a gauze curtain.

Quakers did not approve of bright colors. The women wore plain gray dresses that reached to the floor. Their hair was brushed up in a simple fashion, without curls or any elaborate hair style. When they went out, they wore plain caps over their hair and aprons over their dresses.

Quaker men wore coats and breeches of dark homespun cloth. They wore round hats that were supposed to be set perfectly straight on their heads, and they cut their hair round. Quakers did not wear wigs or powder their hair. Quaker boys of all ages dressed exactly like their fathers, and girls exactly like their mothers.

Some Philadelphia Quakers had broken away from the traditional gray dress. Some women had begun to wear blue or yellow skirts. They even wore frills around their necks! Quaker men were sometimes known to tilt their round hats a trifle instead of wearing them straight!

Benjamin Franklin was not a Quaker, but he dressed much like one. He usually wore a plain brown homespun suit, with no embroidery or decoration whatever.

In contrast to the dress of fashionable people and wealthy Quakers, the poor people

The young Philadelphia Quakers in this family are dressed more stylishly than their parents.

of Philadelphia wore coarse homespun clothes. Usually these were gray, trimmed with black. Men sometimes wore leather coats or leather breeches that would last for many, many years. Both men and women managed to add bright colors to their costumes by wearing large printed handkerchiefs around their necks.

Keeping clean in those days was a real problem. Floor-length skirts became dirty very quickly and so did white lace cuffs and ruffles. To keep from spilling food on clothes when eating, it was the fashion to use a very large napkin, called a "serviette." This was tied around the neck, covering the lace ruffles of a gentleman's shirt front, or the kerchief a lady had pinned across her chest.

Lace cuffs, ruffles, and kerchiefs could be removed from heavier garments for more frequent washing. But laundering was a long, slow process. Water had to be heated in great kettles hung in the fireplace. Soap was usually made by hand from ashes and grease. Ironing was done with "sadirons" heated in the open fire or on a Franklin stove. The iron's handle became as hot as the iron itself, and thick pads or gloves were used to prevent burns on the hands.

If it was difficult to keep one's clothes clean,
it was just as hard to keep one's body clean.
In the homes of the poor, the washstand usually
stood outside the back door. In the winter it
was necessary to break the ice in the water
pail before one could wash.

In the homes of the wealthy, washstands
were inside the bedrooms. But the water would
be almost as icy in the winter. It is easy to
understand why most people did not keep very
clean.

In some homes people took baths every Saturday night. Water was carried from the well, heated over the open fire, and poured into the washtub, which was set in front of a fireplace. The members of the family took turns washing. Filling and emptying the tub was hard work, and hot water was precious. In large families, several children might use the same bath water.

In most homes, however, baths were rare and daily washing very sketchy. Many people preferred to wear perfume rather than wash with cold water and strong soap. The perfume hid unpleasant odors.

Benjamin Franklin had many ideas that people of his day considered foolish. He liked to bathe frequently. He had a copper bathtub, and he would sit in hot water and read. He believed that the hot water eased his pain and that cleanliness was good for him.

Franklin had never been as fond of dancing and the theater as George Washington was. But he was an excellent swimmer, and he had taught many young Philadelphians to swim in the Delaware and the Schuylkill rivers. Rich and poor alike swam whenever they could, all summer long.

Delaware River skaters may have played an early
type of ice hockey like the game these boys are enjoy-
ing in *Skating Scene* by John Toole.

The Quakers approved of swimming, and
they also liked to skate. In the wintertime,
Philadelphia's many ponds froze solid, and the
ice on the Delaware River was often two feet
thick. Then hundreds of people turned out for
ice skating. Sometimes a big fire was built
on the riverbank, and an ox was roasted over
it. People came up to the fire to warm themselves and get something to eat.

Philadelphia children enjoyed swimming, skating, and fishing. They had other favorite pastimes too. Most boys liked to play "shinny," a form of hockey. "Pecking eggs," "plugging tops," and "Duck on Davy" were other popular games. Girls were not encouraged to play outdoors. They were supposed to stay in the house and do needlework.

From the time they were small, girls were trained to be good housewives. They had to learn how to comb, card, dye, and spin wool and flax, and how to knit and sew. They had to learn how to preserve, pickle, cook, bake, make soap, and wash clothes. Even if a housewife had servants she must know how to do all these things properly, and girls began to learn while they were very young.

Every little girl had to make a "sampler," showing the different stitches she could make. Probably Franklin's two little granddaughters worked hard each day that summer on their samplers, as did Washington's adopted granddaughter at Mount Vernon.

6. A Market of Brothers

On May 25, two weeks after Washington arrived in Philadelphia, the Constitutional Convention got started at last. Washington was elected president of the meeting, and the delegates who were present settled down to work. They decided that everything said and done inside the State House should be kept secret.

After that, George Washington took his daily walk to the State House earlier in the morning, and did not come back until late afternoon or evening. Benjamin Franklin was carried to the State House every morning in his sedan chair and home again when the meeting was over.

"The Great Little Madison," as his friends called James Madison, often went home with Franklin instead of returning to the Indian Queen Tavern around the corner. The oldest delegate and one of the youngest had many long talks.

Several times Franklin invited a number of delegates to dinner. His daughter Sarah did not mind. She was used to serving dinner to a dozen or even two dozen guests in the big dining room below her father's library.

Four o'clock was the fashionable hour for dinner, but many people ate earlier. We have records of several Philadelphia dinners of that time. A few years earlier John Adams, who became the second President of the United States, had written that he had been offered at a single meal:

"Duck, ham, chicken, beef, pig, tarts, creams, jellies, sweatmeats of twenty sorts, trifles, floating islands, etc., with a dessert of fruit, raisins, almonds, pears and peaches."

A French visitor described a "simple meal" in the home of a wealthy Quaker in this way:

"The first course consisted of a large piece of beef placed at one end of the table, a ham placed in the middle, a leg of lamb at the other, two soups, four dishes of potatoes, cabbage, vegetables, etc., as well as cider, porter, and beer . . .

"The second course consisted merely of various kinds of pies and cakes, two bowls of cream, two dishes of cheese, and two of butter."

Not everyone had so much to eat, of course. But most Philadelphians had "fine wheat bread, good meats and fowls," and they could have vegetables and fruits that were plentiful.

Children might eat with their parents when there were guests, but they had to be quiet. A book of rules for the behavior of children told them not to speak unless they were spoken to, not to ask for anything at the table, not to take salt "except with a clean knife," and not to throw bones under the table.

Often the children had to sit at a side table. If there were not enough chairs, they stood up to eat.

Cooking was done in the kitchen fireplace, which had a brick oven at one side for baking. Once a week, or when a dinner party was being given, a great fire of dry wood was built inside the oven. The fire was kept burning until all the bricks were very hot. Then the coals and ashes were swept out of the oven, and it was filled with bread, pies, cakes, and anything else that was to be baked. These things were set in the back of the hot oven with a long-handled shovel, called a "peel."

Breakfast, as well as dinner, was a big meal. There might be roast veal or mutton, besides eggs and ham, and hot breads and tea. George Washington ate a small breakfast. He liked to have hoecakes, honey and tea, with perhaps a slice of cold tongue or ham.

At other meals, Washington probably enjoyed the dishes for which Philadelphia was famous, such as oysters, fish, cinnamon buns, scrapple, and pepper pot soup. He certainly saw women trundling carts with soup kettles through the streets and calling out, "Pepper pot! Old-time pepper pot!"

Undoubtedly Washington enjoyed the new dessert, ice cream. With the beginning of the summer heat, the ice-cream man would appear on the street with his trundlebarrow. He would cry out, "R-r-rah, la, la, la! Here's lemon ice cream and vanilla, too!" Dozens of children would run to meet him, each carrying a cup and a spoon for the delicious sweet.

There was no refrigeration, nor were there ice-making machines. In order to have ice cream in the summer, ice had to be cut in the winter from frozen rivers and streams. Then it was packed in sawdust, and stored in icehouses or in cellars. In a letter to his plantation manager that summer of 1787, George Washington wrote careful directions for building a better icehouse at Mount Vernon.

Benjamin Franklin had always had a large vegetable garden. But the year before the Constitutional Convention met, he wrote to a friend that he did not need a garden, because "our well-furnished, plentiful market is the best of gardens."

Franklin referred to the public market of Philadelphia, which was right in front of his home. This famous market consisted of long

This early morning shopper buys a tasty cut of meat in the marketplace. Conestoga wagons, packed with produce, are parked outside the market.

open buildings set in the middle of High Street, extending from First Street to Fourth.

On Tuesday and Friday evenings the bells of Christ Church were always rung to announce that tomorrow would be market day.

"There go the butter bells!" the children would cry, and they would run to remind their mothers to buy certain things from the market the following day.

Long before the "butter bells" rang out, the roads leading into Philadelphia would be crowded with Conestoga wagons, pulled by four or six horses, bringing produce for the next day's market.

The Conestoga wagon, which is sometimes called a "covered wagon" or "prairie schooner," was the freight car of Pennsylvania. It was a huge, heavy wagon with enormous wheels, sometimes a foot wide! The wagon, shaped something like a boat, was covered with a white cloth top. The body of the wagon was painted a bright-red above and blue below.

The day before market day, country people would load their produce in a Conestoga wagon. Then the whole family piled in, taking blankets and food, for they would sleep overnight in their wagon.

No vehicles or animals were allowed inside the market area, so people parked outside. A certain part of the market was kept for fish, a part for butter and cheese, other areas for vegetables and fruits. In the meat section one could find not only beef, pork, and other ordinary meats, but raccoon, opossum, and bear meat.

Everything was laid out neatly and, as one traveler wrote, everything was "as clean as a dining hall." The country men and women were quiet and polite as they sold their wares, and the city people were quiet and polite as they bought. One visitor said it seemed like "a market of brothers." Although the market-place overflowed with people moving in every direction, there was no bumping or arguing or quarreling. The only sounds to be heard were the buzz of conversation and the ripple of pleasant laughter.

No doubt Franklin's daughter Sarah went to market often that summer, and so did Mrs. Morris. Even the richest Philadelphia women went to market themselves. Ladies would set out from home at dawn, usually on foot. Sometimes they carried baskets for their purchases, but often they were followed by servants with

Philadelphians leisurely make their purchases in the
meat section of the High Street Market.

baskets. Gentlemen went to market too. Washington surely strolled through the market often that summer, and Franklin probably visited it in his sedan chair.

It was customary for a buyer to test butter before purchasing. Farmers often brought in small mounds of butter for sampling. Franklin or Washington might take a coin from his pocket and scoop a bit of butter from the mound and taste it. Many other foods were sampled by the buyers. The sellers sometimes provided a spoon or fork for the purpose.

Two market inspectors strolled around in the market to keep an eye on proceedings. If a pound of butter looked small, they weighed it. If it was the least bit underweight, the butter was seized and given to the hospital.

Making change must have been hard for the clerks. Paper money issued by the Continental Congress was almost worthless. "Not worth a Continental" had became a common saying. It took twenty dollars in Continental money to buy one pound of white lump sugar, and about as much for a pound of coffee!

Each of the thirteen states had its own money. It was difficult to figure out how much a Massachusetts or a Virginia coin was worth in Pennsylvania money. In an almanac for that year two whole pages were filled with instructions on how to change money of the thirteen states "each into all the others, and into English money." Washington, Madison, Hamilton, and the other delegates from different states must have had a hard time shopping in Philadelphia that summer!

7. Leather Aprons

No matter how early Washington and the other delegates went to the State House those June mornings, Philadelphia shops were open and the streets busy.

The streets were not only noisy and smelly, but were bright with color too. The dazzling June sunshine glinted on gaily painted awnings and balconies. It shone on hundreds of colored signs.

There were no street markers in Philadelphia at that time, and no numbers on the

doors of shops or houses. When a stranger asked directions, he was told not to look for a certain street, but to look for a certain sign.

Standing on the corner of a business street, the stranger would see dozens of brightly colored picture-signs swinging in the breeze. Many people could not read or write, so merchants used pictures instead of their names in front of their shops. The stranger might see pictures of hats, wigs, shoes, dresses, books, barrels, clocks, candles, guns, wheels, anchors, bread, and so on.

In addition, he would see the brilliant signs that illustrated the names of taverns. There would be the "The Indian Queen," "A Plume of Feathers," "The Pewter Platter," "The Lion," "The White Horse," "The Black Horse," "The Three Crowns," "The Lemon Tree," "Noah's Ark," "The Star and Garter," "The Spread Eagle." All of these picture signs were painted in bright colors on wood, and they hung in front of the inns. Some of them had been painted by Philadelphia's finest artists.

The "Franklin Inn" had an excellent portrait of Benjamin Franklin, with this verse underneath:

"Come view your patriot Father!
    And your Friend,
    And toast to Freedom and to
    slavery's end."

Another tavern displayed this verse:

"I, William McDermott, lives here;
    I sells good porter, ale, and beer;
    I've made my sign a little wider
    To let you know I sell good cider."

Many a shopkeeper lived above his shop. When Benjamin Franklin was young, he had

I never saw an oft removed tree, nor yet an oft removed family that did so well as those that settled be.

This House to Lett

Three removes are as bad as a fire; and a rolling stone gathers no moss.

This old engraving illustrates a proverb from *Poor Richard's Almanack*, written by Franklin and printed in his New Printing Office in 1733.

a printing shop, and for many years he lived upstairs. In the morning it was a simple matter to go to work. He merely got up, had his breakfast, and then went downstairs to his printing press and his shop. The post office of Philadelphia was located in Franklin's shop.

A shop might carry many other things besides the item pictured in the sign over the door. Here is a partial list of the things that

74

could be bought in Franklin's "New Printing Office" soon after it opened:

leather-bound books	Spanish wine
stationery	linseed oil
slates and pencils	coffee and chocolate
ink and ink powder	compasses and scales
sealing wax	Rhode Island cheese
lead pencils	patent medicines
quills for pens	black broadcloth
inkhorns	white stockings
sandglasses	spectacles

When Franklin and his wife were young, Mrs. Franklin often waited on customers in the shop. For years Franklin wore the leather apron that was the badge of a workingman. His club, the "Junto," was often laughingly called the "Leather Apron Club," because most of its members were workingmen.

Later on, as his business grew, Franklin hired some journeymen printers to operate his printing press. Then he discarded his apron.

Franklin also had two or three apprentices, or pupils, to be trained in the business. There were no schools that taught printing or tailoring or weaving. Boys learned a trade by being apprenticed to a master craftsman. Franklin had been apprenticed at the age of twelve to his older brother who was a printer.

An apprentice promised to serve faithfully, keep his master's secrets, and obey his commands. He could not marry without his master's consent, nor could he leave him. In return, the master promised to give the boy "sufficient meat, drink, clothes, lodging and washing, fitting for an apprentice."

When he finished his term, an apprentice was called a journeyman. Many journeymen

Pat Lyon at the Forge and his apprentice were typical of the craftsmen of Philadelphia.

stayed on to work for wages in the shops where they had been apprenticed.

An apprentice usually thought the term of his apprenticeship much too long. But when he became a journeyman, he was jealous of all apprentices. He thought they would take his job when they finished their training. So the journeymen formed themselves into clubs which we would call trade unions. These clubs tried to get longer terms for apprentices and better wages and shorter hours for journeymen.

The year before the Constitutional Convention met, the journeymen printers of Philadelphia went on strike. They demanded a wage of six dollars a week and got it. A few years later, journeymen carpenters struck for a ten-hour working day, but they lost. In those days people were expected to work twelve to fourteen hours a day.

Many men, women, and children came to America in those days as bond servants. Before leaving Europe, they signed contracts promising to work without wages in America for a certain number of years, usually three to seven. Parents sometimes sold their children as bond servants, in order to pay their own passage to America!

Both Washington and Franklin had had several bond servants. They worked side by side with the apprentices and learned the same trade. When their term of service was up, they, too, might stay and work for wages.

In some homes, bond servants were treated cruelly. Sometimes a bond servant would run away. If he was caught, he was usually flogged, perhaps tied to a whipping post.

The stock, the pillory, and the whipping post stood in the upper part of Philadelphia's marketplace. The stock was a wooden frame with holes in which the hands and feet of the prisoner were fastened. The pillory was attached to a tree or a post, and the offender's head and hands were securely fastened in it.

Passersby often laughed at the people who were being punished. Small boys threw rotten fruit at them. Spending a day in either stock or pillory was a most unpleasant experience.

Since Benjamin Franklin had become the President of Pennsylvania, some of its laws had been changed. Only murderers and traitors could now be hanged. Before that, a person could be hanged merely for stealing a loaf of bread! It was against the law now to brand a criminal with a hot iron or to cut off his ears. Many people considered that these new laws were too lenient!

Frequently Franklin had urged the people of Philadelphia to set up a small police force. Now property owners were taxed according to the value of their land, and the money was used to pay the market inspectors and night watchmen.

All night long watchmen walked the streets. They called out the hour and the weather: "Ten o'clock and all's well! Clear and warm."

And Franklin, Washington, Madison, Hamilton, and the other Constitutional Convention delegates, who usually went to bed early like most Philadelphians, knew that tomorrow would be another hot day.

8. "Fire!"

"Fire! Fire!"

During the summer of the Constitutional Convention, Washington must have heard this cry of the night watchman.

George Washington and Robert Morris surely dressed and ran to the scene of the fire.

Benjamin Franklin, too old now for fire fighting, probably stayed in bed and listened. Through his open bedroom window, he could hear the clang of the State House bell and the chime of the Christ Church bells. He heard people running and shouting. He heard the clatter of wheels as men pulled the little fire engine along the street.

80

Franklin had been to so many fires that he could picture the scene clearly. He could see fire fighters running toward the blazing house carrying leather buckets and stout linen bags. He could see men dashing into the burning house and out again, carrying clothes and other property in their bags. He could see flames licking at the roof, and he could smell smoke and scorching wood and paint. He could hear the crackle of the flames and the hiss of steam as the water met the fire.

There were no fire hoses and no hydrants. There was merely a hand pump on a simple

When Ben Franklin (left) was young, he fought fires with an engine like this one. The fire fighters used buckets to fill it with water. Others pressed down the pump handles to send the water out of the nozzle.

Men poised on top of fire engines direct the nozzles
toward the flames in this three-alarm fire.

fire engine. The buckets of the fire fighters
kept the engine supplied with water.

A double line of people quickly formed from
the burning building to the nearest river, pond,
or well. Leather fire buckets were filled with
water and passed from hand to hand in the
"water line." The water was poured into the
little engine and pumped on the fire. The
empty buckets were passed down the other
line, which was called the "dry line." This line
was usually made up of boys and women.

No idle bystanders were allowed. If anyone
tried to stand aside and watch, people in both
lines would cry out, "Fall in! Fall in!"

82

If the bystander did not fall in line at once and help, somebody was sure to empty a full bucket of water on his head!

Philadelphia had the best fire-fighting organization of the day. Benjamin Franklin had boasted recently, "The city has never lost by fire more than one or two houses at a time." This was unusual. In most cities a fire was apt to get out of control and sweep through several city blocks.

Franklin had a right to boast, because he was largely responsible for Philadelphia's freedom from fire damage. He had formed the very first organized volunteer fire fighters in America fifty years earlier. He remembered their training meetings. Each member had six water buckets and two stout linen bags for salvage. These buckets and bags were always kept by the fire fighter's front door. When an alarm was sounded, he snatched up buckets and bags and ran to the fire.

When Franklin heard people returning home, he knew that the fire had been put out. Buckets and bags would be hung on street posts until morning, when the owners would claim them.

Franklin had also suggested the formation

These are the fire marks of the Green Tree (left) and
the Hand-in-Hand (right) Fire Companies.

of the first fire insurance company in America.
This was known as the "Hand-in-Hand." A
house owner joined the company for seven
years and paid a certain deposit. He was
given a badge, or fire mark, showing "four
hands united." This fire mark was placed high
on the outside front wall of his house.

Soon another fire insurance company, the
"Green Tree," was formed, and its fire mark,
a tree, was placed on members' houses.

Each insurance company had its own fire-fighting brigade. When an alarm was sounded, both fire brigades would run to the fire. The members of the fire brigade whose sign was posted would fight the fire. The others would turn around and go home to bed! The building could burn down for all they cared!

Fire was not the only danger to Philadelphians. A "Humane Society" was formed which placed signs near ferries and popular picnic places. These signs told where hooks and nets could be found to help in the rescue of people who were drowning. The signs also told where medicines were kept for those who had been poisoned or had suffered a sunstroke.

Philadelphia was proud of its many doctors. But we would not want them to treat us today! At that time nothing was known of anesthetics. Operations were performed, and legs cut off, while the patients were fully conscious. Germs had never been heard of. It was a rare doctor who thought it important even to wash his hands before operating. No wonder so many patients died!

A doctor's favorite treatment was apt to be "bloodletting." He would open a patient's vein and take out a cup or two of blood. Bloodletting was often done by barbers. Other cures were "purging, bathing with vinegar, sweating, and blistering the patient from head to foot."

Many Philadelphia women did their own family doctoring. They prepared their own medicines by drying certain weeds, berries, and herbs.

No one knew that mosquitoes carried yellow fever and malaria. Mosquitoes were allowed to breed in the many swamps and ponds around the city. In the dreadful summer heat they were terrible pests. It was no wonder that yellow fever epidemics swept Philadelphia from time to time, and malaria was bad every summer. The favorite treatments for these illnesses were quinine and drastic bleeding.

Smallpox, and tuberculosis, called "consumption," were common diseases. Vaccination had not yet been discovered, but Benjamin Franklin favored "inoculation," and urged it on his friends. This was a method of giving a person a light case of the disease. Washington did not need to be inoculated, because he had had smallpox when he was a young man, and could not get it again. His face was badly pitted from the dreadful disease.

We would consider the Philadelphia of that day a very unsanitary city. Ditches and creeks, full of sewage, emptied into the rivers. Doctors did not understand that these open sewers were dangerous to health.

Philadelphia's finest doctors believed that night air was bad for the health. People were warned to sleep with their windows closed. Doctors also urged their patients to wear nightcaps in bed to keep from getting colds and toothaches.

Benjamin Franklin did not believe that night air was any more dangerous than any other air. He slept with his windows open, and when he rode in a carriage he opened the curtains to let in fresh air.

9. "A Rising Sun"

George Washington, president of the Constitutional Convention, rose from the speaker's chair in the State House of Philadelphia to stand in front of the members. It was Monday, September 17, 1787.

"You have heard Dr. Franklin's motion," Washington said, "that we accept this Constitution for the United States of America. I hope this motion will prevail and we can consider our work here finished."

The delegates then voted on Franklin's motion, and the Constitution was accepted. One by one the members came forward to sign it.

For four months the delegates had worked on the Constitution. Throughout the long hot summer they had met every day, all day long. Sometimes they sat so late that candles had to be brought in for light.

It had been very difficult to make a plan of government that all the states would accept. Nobody was entirely satisfied with the finished Constitution. Each state had had to give in on some points. But most of the delegates agreed that it was the best they could do.

Delegates to the Convention sign the Constitution. Washington presides; Franklin is seated at the left.

There had been hot arguments and furious quarrels among the delegates as they worked on the Constitution. George Washington often had to pound his gavel so hard that he made the big silver inkstand jump. Benjamin Franklin did his best to keep peace, but it wasn't easy.

James Madison kept a journal all during the Convention. He wrote down every word that was said. Since he was a frequent speaker as well, he was a very busy man.

As the weary delegates signed the Constitution, Benjamin Franklin kept looking at the speaker's chair. On its high back was a carving of a sun, either rising or setting.

As the last member signed, Franklin said, "I have often and often in the course of the session . . . looked at that sun behind the president without being able to tell whether it was rising or setting. But now at length I have the happiness to know that it is a rising and not a setting sun."

The wise old man was right. The sun of the United States of America was rising. The Constitution, which the Convention wrote, is still the law of our land, the foundation of our nation. It has lasted nearly 200 years.

This engraved plate by Amos Doolittle was a tribute
to George Washington and the United States.

That evening George Washington wrote in his diary:

> "The business being thus closed, the Members adjourned to the City Tavern, dined together, and took a cordial leave of each other.
> "Then I retired to think about the momentous work which had been executed, after not less than five . . . and sometimes seven hours sitting every day . . . for more than four months."

The next day Washington made farewell calls on his Philadelphia friends, including Benjamin Franklin.

When Washington rose to leave his old friend, he looked down at the fat, aging figure in the unique armchair. He remembered all the things that Benjamin Franklin had done in his long and active life. He had been printer, scientist, inventor, journalist, lawmaker, businessman, and philosopher. He had reorganized the post office system of the American colonies. He had done many, many things for the betterment of Philadelphia and his country.

"It must please you, sir," Washington said to the wise old man, "to know that you have not lived in vain. I will always remember you with respect and affection."

For once Benjamin Franklin could not think of a joke. This tribute from General Washington he would treasure the rest of his life.

Glossary

apprentice: one who is learning a trade by working for a skilled tradesman

armonica: a musical instrument invented by Franklin, played by rubbing fingers against rotating half-globes of glass

bifocals: eyeglasses with lenses which have two parts—one for near and one for far vision

busybody: a double-paned mirror fastened to a window sill which enabled a person indoors to see outdoors without being seen

butter bells: church bells which were rung the evening before a market day

clothespress: a large chest in which clothes may be hung

cobblestones: round stones used in paving streets

commode: a washstand which has a cupboard underneath it

"contrivances": the name which Benjamin Franklin gave to his many inventions

flax: a blue-flowered plant, the fibers of which may be spun into linen thread

footscraper: a bar fixed to the doorstep of a house for removing mud from shoes

homespun: a loosely-woven woolen or linen fabric

inoculation: the injection into the body of a serum that will prevent a person from getting a disease

journeyman: a young man who has been an apprentice and now works for himself or a craftsman

mangle: the machine invented by Franklin for ironing laundry by passing it between rollers

minuet: a slow, graceful dance

necessary: a toilet

ordinary: an inn or a tavern

peel: a long-handled shovel used to place food to be baked in a fireplace oven

pillory: a wooden frame with holes in which a prisoner's head and hands were locked

postrider: a man who delivered mail by horseback

quadrille: a slow square dance for four couples

rigging: the ropes used to hold up and work the masts and sails of a ship

sadiron: a flatiron pointed at both ends

sampler: a decorative piece of cloth that is hand-embroidered

serviette: a large table napkin

setting pole: a long pole used for pushing boats along in the shallow water of a stream

stock: a wooden frame with holes in which the hands and feet of a prisoner could be locked

winch: a machine used to hoist or to pull by means of a drum turned by a crank

94

Index

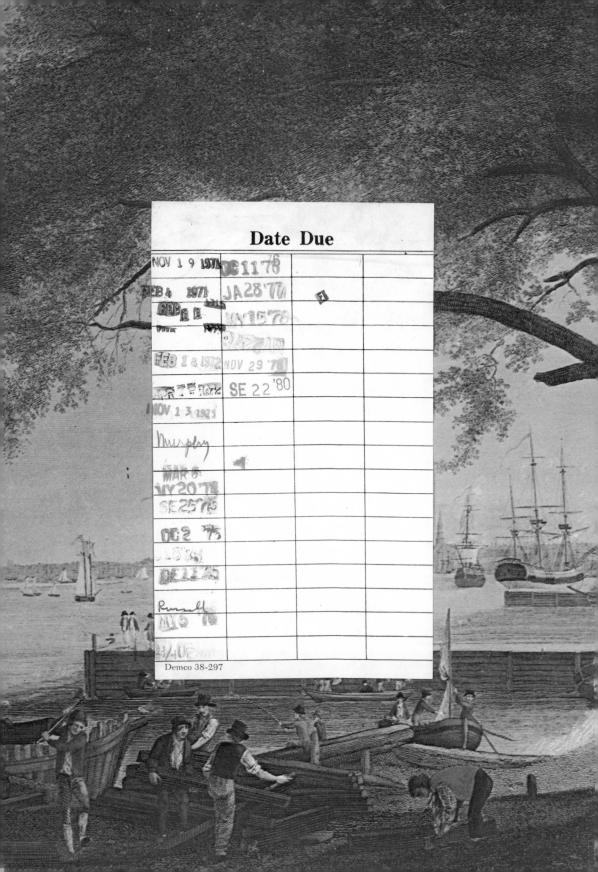